Dictionary of
GEOGRAPHICAL
TERMS

By Margaret Lysecki
and Jon Murray

CELEBRATION PRESS

The following people from **Pearson Learning Group**
have contributed to the development of this product:

Joan Mazzeo, Jennifer Visco **Design** | **Editorial** Betsy Niles, Donna Garzinsky
Christine Fleming **Marketing** | **Publishing Operations** Jennifer Van Der Heide
Production Laura Benford-Sullivan
Content Area Consultant Dr. Linda Greenow

The following people from **DK** have
contributed to the development of this product:

Art Director Rachael Foster

Keith Davis, Carole Oliver **Design** | **Managing Editor** Scarlett O'Hara
Carlo Ortu **Picture Research** | **Editorial** Ben Hoare, Kate Pearce
Ed Merritt **Cartography** | **Production** Rosalind Holmes
Richard Czapnik, Andy Smith **Cover Design** | **DTP** David McDonald
Consultant David Green

Dorling Kindersley would like to thank: Johnny Pau for additional cover design work.

Picture Credits: Corbis: 8bl; ABC Basin Ajansi 19tr; Jonathan Andrew 14br; Peter Beck 11tl; Yann Arthus Bertrand 9bl; Pablo Corral 26tr; Ric Ergenbright 10bl; Fritz Polking/Frank Lane Picture Agency 26l; Arne Hodalic 27br; Dave G. Houser 5bl; Bob Krist 23tr; Lester Lefkowitz 27tr; Danny Lehman 1; Charles O'Rear 24bl; Jose Fuste Raga 7bl; Galen Rowell 19tl, 21bl; Grant Smith 13tl; James A. Sugar 30tr; Paul A. Souders 16bl, 25bl; S. Feval/Le Matin/Corbis Sygma 6cl; SYGMA 29br; Craig Tuttle 22bl.DK Images: Joe Cornish 30bl; Brian Cosgrove 17cr; Stephen Oliver 10br. Getty Images: 27bl; Tony Craddock 25br; John Kelly 9tr; Frans Lemmens 4tr, 25cl; NASA 12cl; Zigy Kaluzny 10tr. Ben Hoare: 9tr. Science Photo Library: Alan Sirulnikoff 28bl; Bernhard Edmaier 23bl; Martin Bond 6bl, 24br; Simon Fraser 12tr, 29tr; Tom McHugh 12br; Worldstat International 22tr.

All other images: DK Dorling Kindersley © 2005. For further information see www.dkimages.com

ISBN: 0-7652-5218-X

Color reproduction by Colourscan, Singapore
Printed in the United States of America
3 4 5 6 7 8 9 10   08 07 06 05 04

1-800-321-3106
www.pearsonlearning.com

Contents

What Is Geography?

Geography is a word that comes from ancient Greece. The Greek root *geo* means "Earth." The root *graph* means "writing."

When you study geography, you study many things. You study Earth's land and water and its climate and weather. You also observe where people live and how groups of people interact with the environment. Geography also teaches about Earth's environmental changes and the issues and problems these changes may present.

There are special words or terms that are used to understand geography. This dictionary will help explain what some of those words mean. It will also help in spelling and pronouncing the words.

rain forest

hurricane

Shiprock, New Mexico, is a type of hill called a mesa.

Using the Dictionary

On each page of this dictionary, you will see entry words listed in alphabetical order. Each entry word has a definition. Next to each entry word, in parentheses, is its pronunciation. When you read the pronunciation out loud, you will learn how to say the entry word correctly.

At the top of each page you will see two guide words. They are the first and last entry words on the page. Any word that comes in alphabetical order between the guide words may be on the page.

guide words —

alphabet —

entry word —

definition —

pronunciation —

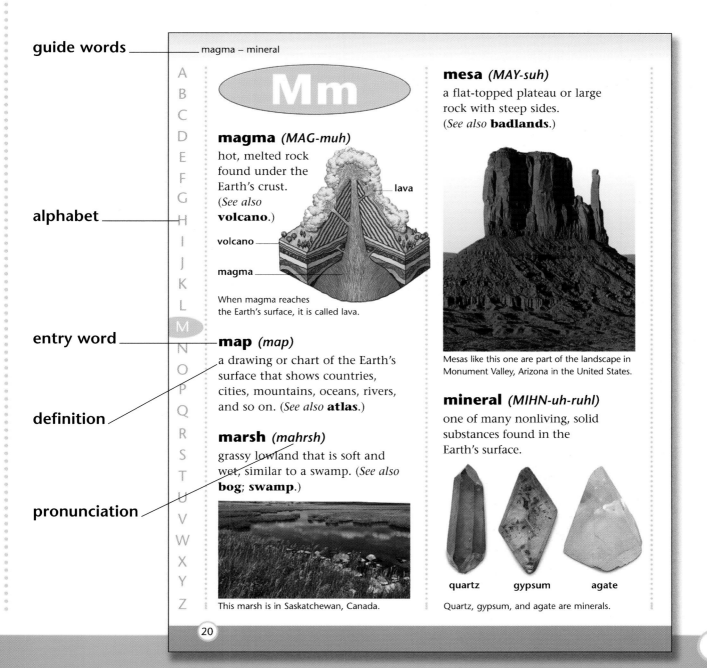

magma – mineral

Mm

magma *(MAG-muh)*
hot, melted rock found under the Earth's crust. *(See also volcano.)*

lava

volcano

magma

When magma reaches the Earth's surface, it is called lava.

map *(map)*
a drawing or chart of the Earth's surface that shows countries, cities, mountains, oceans, rivers, and so on. *(See also atlas.)*

marsh *(mahrsh)*
grassy lowland that is soft and wet, similar to a swamp. *(See also bog; swamp.)*

This marsh is in Saskatchewan, Canada.

mesa *(MAY-suh)*
a flat-topped plateau or large rock with steep sides. *(See also badlands.)*

Mesas like this one are part of the landscape in Monument Valley, Arizona in the United States.

mineral *(MIHN-uh-ruhl)*
one of many nonliving, solid substances found in the Earth's surface.

quartz   gypsum   agate

Quartz, gypsum, and agate are minerals.

20

A B C D E F G H I J K L M N O P Q R S T U V W X Y Z

Aa

altitude *(AL-tih-tood)*

the distance above Earth's surface. The term *altitude* is used for objects that are very tall or high up, such as mountains or airplanes. (*See also* **elevation**; **sea level**.)

This helicopter and hot-air balloon are at a higher altitude than the mountains.

aqueduct *(AK-wuh-dukt)*

a large pipe or channel used to carry water from one place to another.

This aqueduct is in California in the United States.

arid *(AIR-ihd)*

dry. It refers to a region with little rainfall and not much plant life. (*See also* **desert**; **savanna**.)

atlas *(AT-liss)*

a book of maps.

atmosphere *(AT-mus-fihr)*

the layer of gases that surrounds Earth.

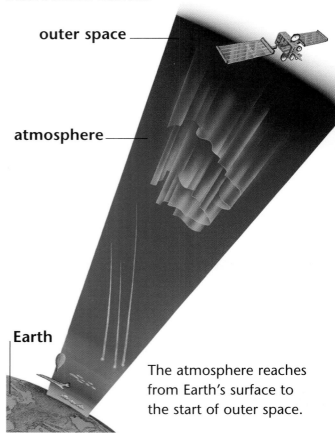

outer space

atmosphere

Earth

The atmosphere reaches from Earth's surface to the start of outer space.

avalanche *(AV-uh-lanch)*

a large mass of snow, earth, or rock that slides rapidly downhill. An avalanche can bury anything in its path.

Bb

badlands *(BAD-landz)*

a dry region where rocks have been worn away to form sharp ridges, peaks, cliffs, and flat-topped mesas. (*See also* **mesa**.)

barrier island
(BAIR-ee-er EYE-land)

a long, thin, sandy island that lies a short distance away from the main coastline. The barrier island protects the coastline from strong waves and currents.

This barrier island lies just off the coast of Tahiti in the Pacific Ocean.

barrier reef *(BAIR-ee-er reef)*

a long, narrow, underwater ridge that is made up of coral, the skeletons of tiny sea animals. It is separated from land by deeper water called a lagoon.

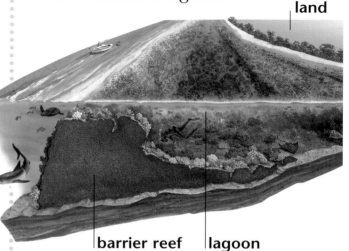

land

barrier reef | lagoon

This diagram shows how a barrier reef is separated from land.

bay *(bay)*

a body of salt water that is connected to the sea or ocean, and is surrounded on three sides by land. (*See also* **inlet**.)

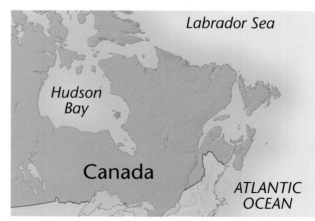

Labrador Sea

Hudson Bay

Canada

ATLANTIC OCEAN

Hudson Bay, Canada, is one of the largest bays in the world.

A B C D E F G H I J K L M N O P Q R S T U V W X Y Z

7

A
B
C
D
E
F
G
H
I
J
K
L
M
N
O
P
Q
R
S
T
U
V
W
X
Y
Z

bayou *(BY-yoo)*

a slow-moving body of water that leads into or out of a lake or a river. *Bayou* is a term used in the southeastern United States.

beach *(beech)*

an area of sand and small stones at the edge of a lake, an ocean, or another body of water.

This is a sandy beach in Western Australia.

bog *(bahg)*

wet, spongy ground. (*See also* **marsh**; **swamp**.)

Bogs, like this one at Rannoch in Scotland, are wet and muddy places.

border *(BOR-dur)*

the line that divides one country or state from another country or state. Some borders are natural, such as rivers or mountains. Other borders can only be seen on a map.

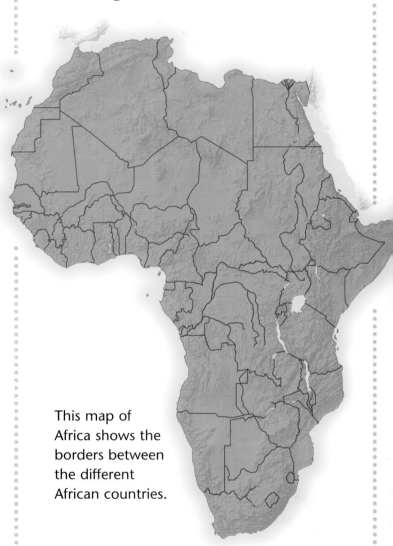

This map of Africa shows the borders between the different African countries.

boundary *(BOWN-duh-ree)*

the line that marks the outside edge of an area. *Boundary* usually refers to the edge of an area smaller than a country or a state.

caldera lake
(kal-DAIR-uh layk)

a body of water in a volcanic crater. (*See also* **volcano**.)

This caldera lake, known as Viti, is in Iceland.

canal *(kuh-NAL)*

a waterway made by people. A canal is like an artificial river. It allows ships to travel inland or across a narrow strip of land.

The Corinth Canal in Greece was dug in 1893. It is 4 miles long.

canyon *(KAN-yuhn)*

a long, deep, narrow opening with very steep sides. (*See also* **gorge**.)

This is the Paria River Canyon in Utah in the United States.

capital city
(KAP-ih-tuhl SIH-tee)

a city that is the center of government for a country, state, or territory.

London is the United Kingdom's capital city.

A
B
C
D
E
F
G
H
I
J
K
L
M
N
O
P
Q
R
S
T
U
V
W
X
Y
Z

A
B
C
D
E
F
G
H
I
J
K
L
M
N
O
P
Q
R
S
T
U
V
W
X
Y
Z

channel (CHAN-uhl)

a narrow body of water joining two larger bodies of water.

chasm (KAZ-uhm)

a great crack in the Earth, such as a valley, a gorge, or a canyon.

city (SIH-tee)

a large, important town where many people live and work.

cliff (klihf)

a steep and often high slope of rock or soil.

White Cliffs of Dover, England

climate (KLY-muht)

the pattern of weather conditions experienced in a place or region over many years.

coast (kohst)

the place where land meets a sea or ocean.

This photograph shows the Gold Coast along Queensland, Australia.

compass (KUHM-puhs)

an instrument used to show directions.

compass

Which Way?

Earth is a large magnet. The needle on a compass is also a magnet. It is pulled by Earth's magnetism to point toward the North Pole. By reading the needle on a compass, a traveler can find the four major directions: north, south, east, and west.

conservation
(kahn-suhr-VAY-shuhn)

the care, protection, and wise use of the environment and other resources.

Recycling metal cans is an example of conservation.

continent (KAHN-tih-nuhnt)

one of the Earth's seven large masses of land.

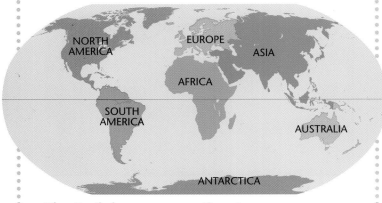

The Earth has seven continents.

cordillera (kohr-dihl-YAIR-uh)

a very large chain of mountains or mountain ranges. It is sometimes the main mountain range of a country or a continent.

The Dolomites cordillera is in northern Italy.

cyclone (SY-klohn)

a very strong storm with powerful winds that move in a circle around a center of low pressure. When it occurs in the Indian Ocean region, it is known as a tropical cyclone. (See also **hurricane**; **typhoon**.)

This satellite photograph shows a tropical cyclone off the east coast of Madagascar.

A B C D E F G H I J K L M N O P Q R S T U V W X Y Z

A B C D E F G H I J K L M N O P Q R S T U V W X Y Z

Dd

delta *(DEHL-tuh)*

a build-up of clay, sand, and other deposits at the mouth of a river. A delta is shaped like a triangle.

This photograph shows the Nile Delta in Egypt.

desert *(DEH-zert)*

a region where very little rain falls. (*See also* **arid**.)

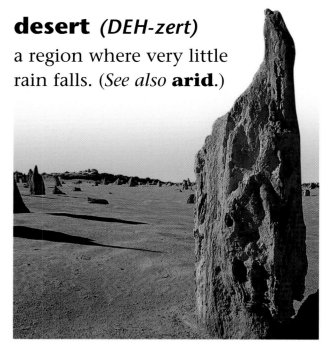

The Pinnacles Desert in Western Australia is named for its strange rock formations.

Many Kinds of Deserts

Deserts may be sandy, like the Sahara Desert in Africa, or rocky, like the Mojave Desert in the United States. Deserts can also be covered in ice and snow, such as the continent Antarctica.

Polar deserts are very dry places in the Arctic, as seen here, and in the Antarctic.

drought *(drowt)*

a long period of little or no rainfall.

This reservoir in California in the United States has dried up because of a severe drought.

Ee

earthquake *(URTH-kwayk)*

a shaking of the Earth's surface.

In 1989, a powerful earthquake damaged many buildings in San Francisco, California, in the United States.

More About Earthquakes

An earthquake is caused by changes that take place below the surface of the Earth. Large areas of rock, called plates, shift or move. The shifting causes the Earth's surface to shake. Earthquakes may be very mild to very destructive.

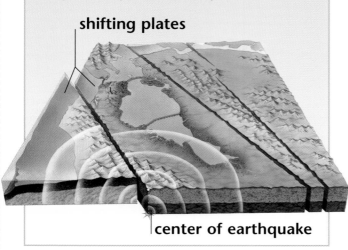

shifting plates

center of earthquake

ecology *(ee-KAHL-uh-gee)*

the study of how living things are connected to each other and to their environment.

ecosystem
(EE-koh-sihs-tuhm)

a system of living things and their environment. In an ecosystem, all the living things affect each other.

A coral reef is an ecosystem. It is home to colorful corals, fish, and other animals.

elevation *(ehl-uh-VAY-shuhn)*

the height of a landform or an object above sea level. (*See also* **altitude**; **sea level**.)

A
B
C
D
E
F
G
H
I
J
K
L
M
N
O
P
Q
R
S
T
U
V
W
X
Y
Z

A
B
C
D
E
F
G
H
I
J
K
L
M
N
O
P
Q
R
S
T
U
V
W
X
Y
Z

environment

(ehn-VY-ruhn-ment)

the physical setting in which plants, animals, and humans live and interact.

Equator *(ih-KWAY-tur)*

an imaginary line around the middle of the Earth. The Equator divides the Earth into the Northern and Southern Hemispheres. (*See also* **hemisphere**.)

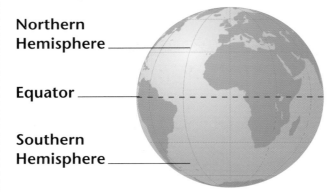

Northern Hemisphere

Equator

Southern Hemisphere

erosion *(ih-ROH-zhuhn)*

the gradual wearing away of the Earth's surface.

Erosion formed this arch in Utah in the United States. The rock was worn away by water.

Many Processes of Erosion

The Earth's surface can be worn away, or eroded, by different processes. Wind and water are the most well-known causes of erosion. Gravity, waves, glaciers, and human actions are other processes that can erode the Earth's surface.

fiord *(fyord)*

a long, deep inlet of the sea with steep, mountainous sides or cliffs. Fiords were formed by the actions of glaciers.

Fiords are very deep and make excellent shelters for ships. This fiord is in Norway.

Gg

geyser *(GY-zur)*

a spring under the ground that shoots streams of hot water and steam high into the air from time to time.

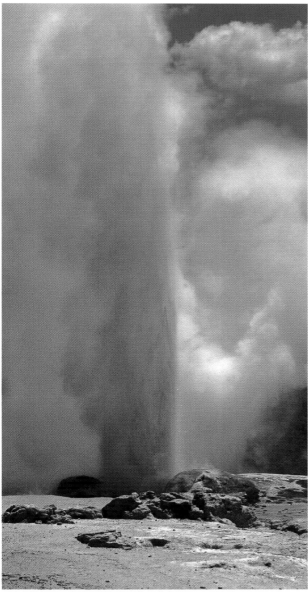

Boiling water and steam rush out of Pohutu Geyser in New Zealand.

glacier *(GLAY-shur)*

a large mass of ice that slowly moves downhill.

This massive glacier is in Alberta, Canada.

global warming *(GLOH-buhl WAR-mihng)*

an increase in the average temperature of Earth's atmosphere. It may be caused by the burning of coal, oil, and gas, which worsens the greenhouse effect. (*See also* **greenhouse effect**.)

globe *(glohb)*

a round model of the Earth showing continents, countries, oceans, and other features.

globe

A
B
C
D
E
F
G
H
I
J
K
L
M
N
O
P
Q
R
S
T
U
V
W
X
Y
Z

A
B
C
D
E
F
G
H
I
J
K
L
M
N
O
P
Q
R
S
T
U
V
W
X
Y
Z

gorge *(gohrj)*

a narrow gap between hills or steep rocks, often with a river flowing through it. (*See also* **canyon**.)

The Gorge du Verdon is in southern France.

grassland *(GRAS-land)*

a wide area of grass-covered land, where few trees grow. Animals often graze there. (*See also* **prairie**; **savanna**.)

Grassland is home to many grazing animals, such as these zebras and impalas in Africa.

greenhouse effect *(GREEN-hows IH-fehkt)*

a warming process that occurs when certain gases in the atmosphere trap the sun's heat for long periods of time. (*See also* **global warming**.)

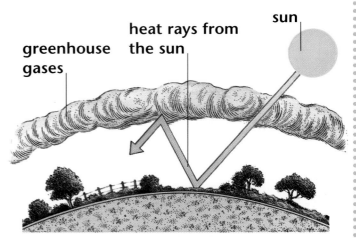

Some gases, called greenhouse gases, trap heat from the sun close to Earth. This heat warms the Earth.

grid *(grihd)*

a pattern of lines that crisscross, forming squares on a globe or map. They are used to help find locations or features on maps and globes. (*See also* **latitude**; **longitude**.)

Grid lines are often marked on maps.

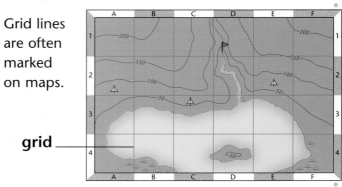

grid

Hh

habitat *(HAB-ih-tat)*

the environment or area where an animal or plant lives.

A pond is a common habitat for frogs.

hemisphere *(HEH-mus-fihr)*

any of the halves of the Earth. The Equator is an imaginary line that divides the Earth into the Northern and Southern Hemispheres. The prime meridian is an imaginary line that divides the Earth into the Eastern and Western Hemispheres.

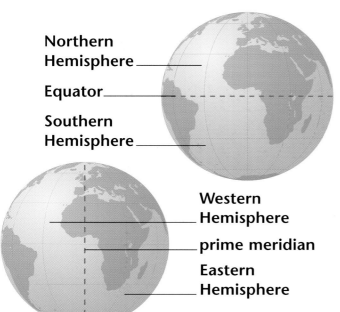

Northern Hemisphere

Equator

Southern Hemisphere

Western Hemisphere

prime meridian

Eastern Hemisphere

humidity *(hyoo-MIHD-uh-tee)*

the amount of water vapor in the atmosphere. Warm air holds more moisture than cool air. Therefore, warm air can be more humid. As warm air rises, the moisture it contains forms droplets which join together to create clouds.

Clouds are a kind of water vapor.

hurricane *(HER-ih-kayn)*

a powerful tropical storm with very high winds. It usually includes heavy rains, thunder, and lightning. Hurricanes usually start in the Atlantic Ocean or the Caribbean Sea. (*See also* **cyclone**; **typhoon**.)

During a hurricane, winds blow at 73 or more miles per hour.

A
B
C
D
E
F
G
H
I
J
K
L
M
N
O
P
Q
R
S
T
U
V
W
X
Y
Z

inlet *(IHN-leht)*

a small bay or stream that runs inland from an ocean or a river. (*See also* **bay**.)

The coast of Scotland has many inlets.

irrigation *(ihr-a-GAY-shun)*

the use of pipes, ditches, or streams to bring water to land for farming.

An irrigation system is being used to help these crops grow in Hanalei Valley, Hawaii in the United States.

island *(EYE-luhnd)*

an area of land, smaller than a continent, that is surrounded on all sides by water.

key *(kee)*

a list that explains the symbols on a map or a chart. The symbols stand for actual places or objects.

Map Key

— State boundary

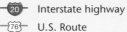 Interstate highway

 U.S. Route

⭐ State capital

◉ Other city

The key can help you to read this map of the state of Georgia in the United States.

lake *(layk)*

a large body of fresh or salt water that is often surrounded by land.

This lake is in the Northwest Territories of Canada.

landform *(LAND-fawrm)*

a shape or structure that is formed naturally on the surface of the Earth. A mountain is one example of a landform.

The Bungle Bungles in Western Australia are an example of a landform.

landslide *(LAND-slyd)*

a mass of soil and rocks that moves quickly down a hill. It can be caused by an earthquake, heavy rain, or the cutting away of the base of a slope.

This landslide in Turkey damaged a road.

latitude *(LAT-ih-tood)*

horizontal grid lines on a map or a globe. Latitude is used to show location north or south of the Equator and is measured in degrees.

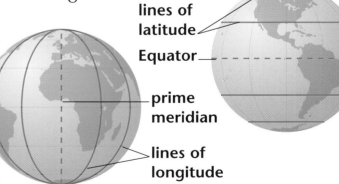

lines of latitude
Equator
prime meridian
lines of longitude

longitude *(LAWN-juh-tood)*

vertical grid lines on a map or a globe. Longitude is used to show location east or west of the prime meridian and is measured in degrees.

A B C D E F G H I J K L M N O P Q R S T U V W X Y Z

A B C D E F G H I J K L **M** N O P Q R S T U V W X Y Z

Mm

magma *(MAG-muh)*

hot, melted rock found under the Earth's crust. *(See also* **volcano**.*)*

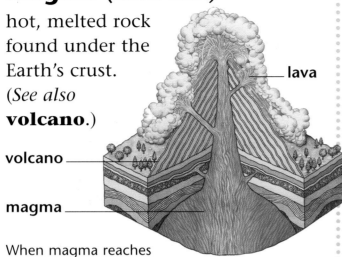

When magma reaches the Earth's surface, it is called lava.

map *(map)*

a drawing or chart of the Earth's surface that shows countries, cities, mountains, oceans, rivers, and so on. *(See also* **atlas**.*)*

marsh *(mahrsh)*

grassy lowland that is soft and wet, similar to a swamp. *(See also* **bog**; **swamp**.*)*

This marsh is in Saskatchewan, Canada.

mesa *(MAY-suh)*

a flat-topped plateau or large rock with steep sides. *(See also* **badlands**.*)*

Mesas like this one are part of the landscape in Monument Valley, Arizona in the United States.

mineral *(MIHN-uh-ruhl)*

one of many nonliving, solid substances found in the Earth's surface.

quartz   gypsum   agate

Quartz, gypsum, and agate are minerals.

monolith (MAHN-uh-lihth)

a huge block of stone, such as Uluru in Australia's Northern Territory.

Uluru lies near the center of the Australian continent. It is 6 miles around at its base.

monsoon (mahn-SOON)

a wind that occurs mainly in the Indian Ocean region and southern Asia. It usually blows from the southwest in summer and from the northeast in winter.

moor (moor)

an area of rolling land that is often covered with heather. Moors can be dry or marshy.

mountain (MOWNT-n)

a landform that rises above its surroundings and is much higher than a hill.

The Matterhorn in Switzerland is one of Europe's tallest mountains.

Nn

nation (NAY-shuhn)

a large community of people living in the same country under the same government.

natural resource (NACH-uhr-uhl REE-sohrs)

a material found in nature that can be used by people and animals. Water, soil, and coal are examples of natural resources. Natural resources may be used to make other things.

kettle   **bricks**   **books**

These everyday items are all made from natural resources.

nonrenewable resource (nahn-rih-NOO-uh-buhl REE-sohrs)

a raw material that is limited in supply. Once it is used up, it cannot be replaced. Crude oil is a nonrenewable resource.

North Pole (north pohl)

the place that is farthest north on the Earth.

A B C D E F G H I J K L M N O P Q R S T U V W X Y Z

A
B
C
D
E
F
G
H
I
J
K
L
M
N
O
P
Q
R
S
T
U
V
W
X
Y
Z

Oo

ocean *(OH-shuhn)*

the large body of salt water that covers three-quarters of Earth's surface. The ocean is all connected, but it is divided into several major areas, including the Atlantic, Pacific, and Indian Oceans.

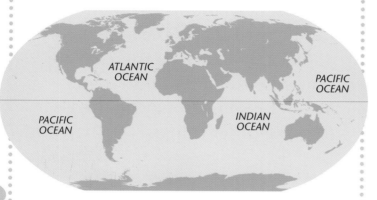

ATLANTIC OCEAN
PACIFIC OCEAN
PACIFIC OCEAN
INDIAN OCEAN

Earth's ocean is divided into several major areas. Some of them are shown on this map.

The ocean provides us with many things, including food and minerals.

Pp

peninsula *(puh-NIHN-suh-luh)*

a piece of land surrounded on three sides by water, or that extends out into a body of water.

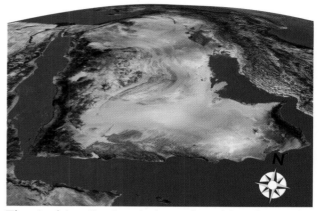

N

The Arabian Peninsula is enclosed by the Red Sea, the Indian Ocean, and the Persian Gulf.

plain *(playn)*

a large area of flat or almost flat land. (*See also* **prairie**.)

Plains are often good for agricultural use. These fields are in Israel.

22

plateau (pla-TOH)

a large, raised landform that is fairly flat or level on top.

This plateau in Arizona in the United States is surrounded by cliffs.

polar climate
(POH-luhr KLY-muht)

a climate that occurs in the areas of the North Pole and the South Pole.

Polar climates are extremely cold.

pollution (puh-LOO-shun)

the dirtying of land, water, or air with harmful substances or materials.

pond (pahnd)

a small body of water. It is either formed naturally or made artificially, such as a pond in a garden.

population
(pahp-yoo-LAY-shuhn)

the total number of people living in an area or country.

China has the world's largest population. This street is in the Chinese city of Shanghai.

Population Table	
China	1,284,304,000
India	1,045,845,000
United States	287,041,000
Indonesia	232,072,000
Brazil	176,030,000
Pakistan	147,663,000
Russia	144,979,000
Bangladesh	133,377,000
Nigeria	129,935,000
Japan	126,975,000
Mexico	103,400,000
Philippines	84,526,000
United Kingdom	59,778,000
Canada	31,902,000
Australia	19,547,000

prairie (PRAIR-ee)

a large, mostly flat, grass-covered area with few or no trees.

A
B
C
D
E
F
G
H
I
J
K
L
M
N
O
P
Q
R
S
T
U
V
W
X
Y
Z

precipitation
(pree-sih-puh-TAY-shuhn)

water droplets or ice crystals that fall from the atmosphere to the ground. Precipitation can fall as mist, drizzle, rain, sleet, hail, or snow.

prime meridian
(prym muh-RIH-dee-uhn)

the line of longitude at 0° that separates the Eastern Hemisphere from the Western Hemisphere. (*See also* **hemisphere**; **longitude**.)

prime meridian

promontory
(PRAH-muhn-tor-ee)

a high ridge of land or rock that sticks out into a body of water.

The Cape of Good Hope is a promontory at the southern tip of the African continent.

province (PRAH-vihnts)

a district or part of a country. It has its own government to decide local matters, but it also answers to the central government of the country. (*See also* **state**.)

provincial city
(proh-VIHN-shuhl SIH-tee)

a city located outside the main population area of a state. A provincial city is the center of a region and provides services to people who live within and near its boundaries.

Qq

quarry (KWOHR-ee)

a place where rock or stone that is used for building material is blasted or cut out of the Earth.

This quarry in Wales is 1,000 feet deep.

Rr

rain forest *(rayn FOHR-uhst)*

an area that is densely forested with tall trees and other vegetation. Rain forests have heavy rainfall throughout the year. Most rain forests are found in the tropics. Rain forests are home to more kinds of plants and animals than any other environment on Earth.

Thick vegetation grows within rain forests, such as this rain forest in Costa Rica.

range *(raynj)*

a row of connected hills or mountains.

The Southern Alps is a mountain range in the South Island of New Zealand.

reservation *(reh-zuhr-VAY-shuhn)*

an area of public land that is set aside for the use of native peoples.

river *(RIH-vuhr)*

a large, natural stream of water that flows into another river, a lake, or an ocean.

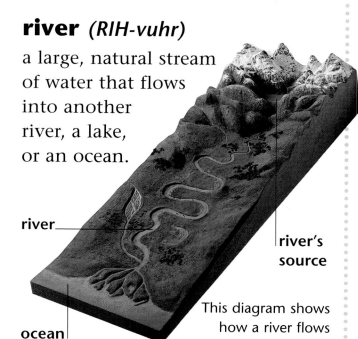

river

river's source

ocean

This diagram shows how a river flows to an ocean.

rural *(ROOR-uhl)*

having to do with areas that are mainly countryside with sparse populations. Farming is often important in these areas. (*See also* **population**; **urban**.)

This photograph shows cows grazing in a rural area in Devon, England.

A B C D E F G H I J K L M N O P Q R S T U V W X Y Z

savanna (suh-VAN-uh)

a grassy plain with a scattering of trees and seasonal rainfall. It is found in places with a tropical or subtropical climate. (*See also* **grassland**.)

This picture shows a savanna in Africa.

sea (see)

a large body of water, usually salt water, that is partly surrounded by land.

sea level (see LEH-vuhl)

the height of the surface of the ocean. Sea level is used to measure the height of an area or a landform. A mountain might be hundreds of feet above sea level; a canyon may be hundreds of feet below sea level.

settlement (SEH-tul-muhnt)

any place to which people have moved to live. Settlements can be large or small, and new or old.

This settlement is on a hillside in Caracas, the capital city of Venezuela in South America.

South Pole (sowth pohl)

the place that is farthest south on Earth.

state (stayt)

an area of land where people have their own government. In the United States, states share power with the federal government. (*See also* **province**.)

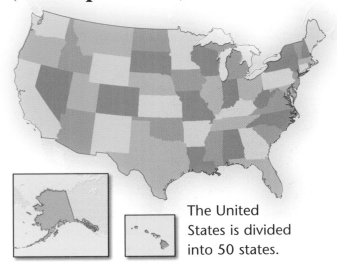

The United States is divided into 50 states.

strait (strayt)

a narrow waterway that connects two larger bodies of water.

The Strait of Gibraltar connects the Atlantic Ocean with the Mediterranean Sea.

stream (streem)

a small body of flowing water, such as a brook or a creek.

This stream runs through a valley in Iceland.

suburb (SU-buhrb)

an area of homes and small businesses that is immediately outside a city.

This suburb is outside of Las Vegas, Nevada, in the United States.

summit (SU-miht)

the top or highest place of a hill or a mountain.

swamp (swahmp)

a wet, soft lowland with trees and plants. (*See also* **bog**; **marsh**.)

This swamp is in Papua New Guinea.

A
B
C
D
E
F
G
H
I
J
K
L
M
N
O
P
Q
R
S
T
U
V
W
X
Y
Z

Tt

temperate climate
(TEHM-puh-riht KLY-muht)

a climate zone that has mild seasons, including warm summers and cool or cold winters. (*See also* **climate**.)

timberline *(TIHM-buhr-lyn)*

the height on a mountain above which trees will not grow due to the harsh climate. Also, the timberline, or tree line, is the distance north or south of the Equator beyond which trees will not grow. (*See also* **Equator**.)

These Canadian mountains are forested below the timberline and bare above it.

tornado *(tohr-NAY-doh)*

a small, violent windstorm with a funnel-shaped cloud. Tornadoes are very destructive.

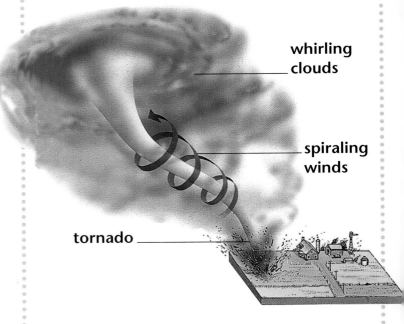

whirling clouds

spiraling winds

tornado

tributary
(TRIHB-yoo-tair-ee)

a stream or river that flows into a larger stream or river.

The tributary on the left joins a much larger river on the right.

A
B
C
D
E
F
G
H
I
J
K
L
M
N
O
P
Q
R
S
T
U
V
W
X
Y
Z

Tropic of Cancer
(TRAH-pihk uhv KAN-suhr)

an imaginary circle around the Earth. This line is 23.5° north of the Equator and is parallel to it.

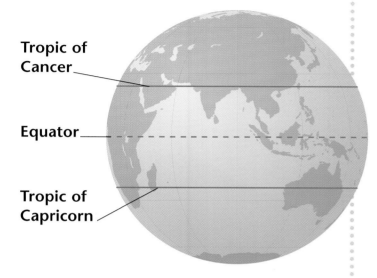

Tropic of Capricorn
(TRAH-pihk uhv KA-prih-kohrn)

an imaginary circle around the Earth. This line is 23.5° south of the Equator and is parallel to it.

tropical climate
(TRAH-pih-kul KLY-muht)

a climate in which it is warm or hot most of the year, with extreme heat and heavy rains in the summer. (*See also* **climate**; **tropics**.)

tropics (TRAH-pihks)

the regions near the Equator; the hottest parts of the Earth.

tundra (TUN-druh)

a vast, treeless area found in Arctic regions. The tundra is mostly flat. Even in the brief summer, the soil is always frozen a few feet below the surface.

Tundra covers much of Greenland.

typhoon (ty-FOON)

a type of tropical storm with high winds and strong rains that forms over the western Pacific Ocean near Asia. (*See also* **cyclone**; **hurricane**.)

Typhoons can cause serious flooding and damage if they reach land.

A
B
C
D
E
F
G
H
I
J
K
L
M
N
O
P
Q
R
S
T
U
V
W
X
Y
Z

urban *(UR-buhn)*

having to do with cities. Urban areas have many people, buildings, traffic, and businesses.

Sydney and its surrounding areas make up the largest urban region in Australia.

valley *(VAL-ee)*

an area of low land that lies between two hills or mountains.

This fertile valley is in Killarney, Ireland.

vegetation *(veh-juh-TAY-shuhn)*

any or all of the plants in a certain area.

volcano *(vahl-KAY-noh)*

an opening in the Earth's crust where lava, rock, gases, and dust are sometimes forced out. (*See also* **magma**.)

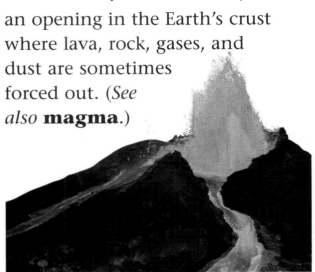

Puu Oo spews molten lava on Big Island, Hawaii, in the United States.

A Peek At Volcanoes

Volcanoes are found on the ocean floor as well as on land. Mt. Pinatubo in the Philippines is an example of a volcano that erupts violently and causes great destruction. Mauna Loa in Hawaii in the United States erupts frequently but usually less violently.

wetland *(WEHT-land)*

area of land that contains marshes or swamps. (*See also* **swamp**.)

Climate Map of the World

This map shows the climate, or normal weather conditions, in each region of the world. Each kind of climate is shown in a different color.

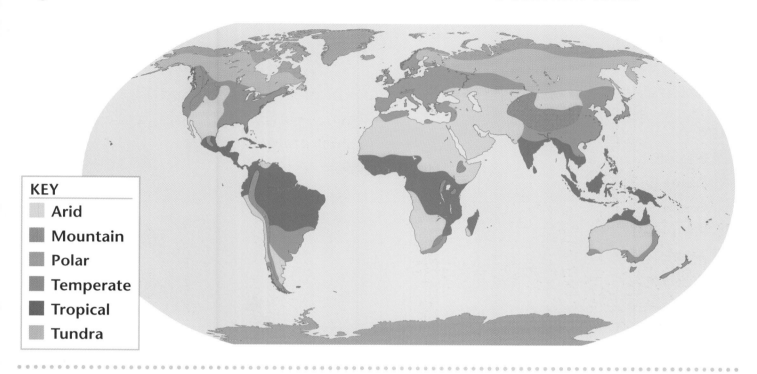

KEY
- Arid
- Mountain
- Polar
- Temperate
- Tropical
- Tundra

Physical Map of the World

On this map, you can see what the height of the land is in different parts of the world.

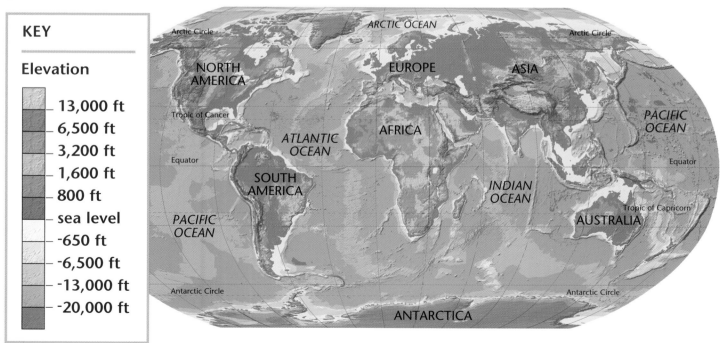

KEY

Elevation

- 13,000 ft
- 6,500 ft
- 3,200 ft
- 1,600 ft
- 800 ft
- sea level
- -650 ft
- -6,500 ft
- -13,000 ft
- -20,000 ft

Language Map of the World

This map shows the main language spoken in many parts of the world.
Each language is shown in a different color.

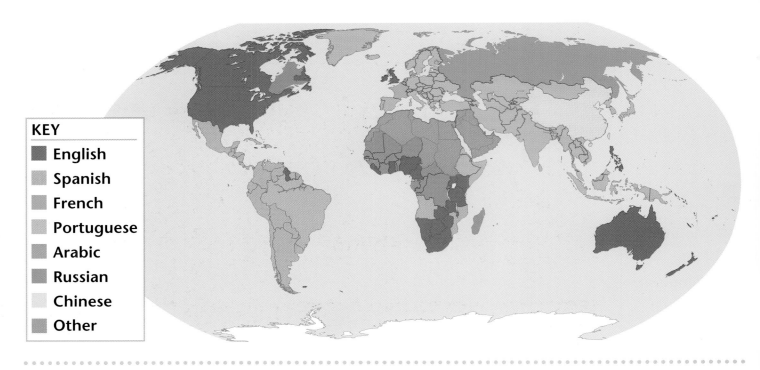

KEY
- English
- Spanish
- French
- Portuguese
- Arabic
- Russian
- Chinese
- Other

Population Map of the World

This map shows the population density, or the number of people living
in each square mile, for different parts of the world.

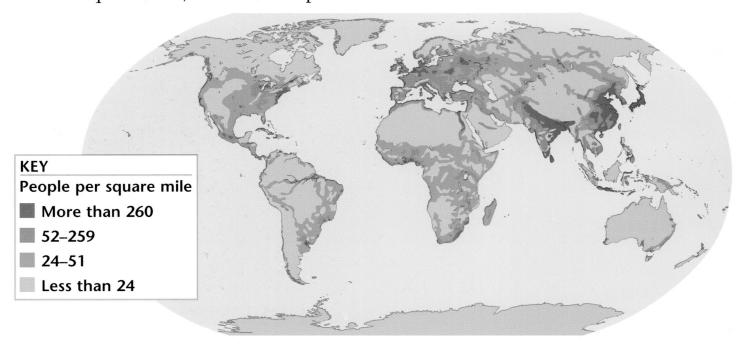

KEY
People per square mile
- More than 260
- 52–259
- 24–51
- Less than 24